P9-ELG-279

CH

FEB   2016
Westminster Public Library
3705 W. 112th Ave.
Westminster, CO 80031
www.westminsterlibrary.org

DISCARD

THE TROPICAL INDIAN OCEAN

Doreen Gonzales

Enslow Elementary

an imprint of

 Enslow Publishers, Inc.

40 Industrial Road
Box 398
Berkeley Heights, NJ 07922
USA

http://www.enslow.com

Enslow Elementary, an imprint of Enslow Publishers, Inc.
Enslow Elementary is a registered trademark of Enslow Publishers, Inc.

Copyright © 2013 by Enslow Publishers, Inc.
All rights reserved.

No part of this book may be reproduced by any means without the written permission of the publisher.

Library of Congress Cataloging-in-Publication Data:
Gonzales, Doreen.
    The tropical Indian ocean / Doreen Gonzales.
      p. cm. — (Our earth's oceans)
    Includes index.
    Summary: "Learn about the Indian Ocean—the animals that call it home, the sea floor, and all of its resources. Also read about the people who have explored it and what is being done to keep the Indian Ocean clean"—Provided by publisher.
    ISBN 978-0-7660-4089-2
    1. Indian Ocean—Juvenile literature. I. Title.
    GC721.G67 2013
    551.46'15—dc23
                    2012007617

Future editions:
Paperback ISBN 978-1-4644-0150-3
ePUB ISBN 978-1-4645-1057-1
Single User PDF ISBN 978-1-4646-1057-8
Multi-User PDF ISBN 978-0-7660-4435-7

Printed in the United States of America
102012Lake Book Manufacturing, Inc., Melrose Park, IL

10 9 8 7 6 5 4 3 2 1

To Our Readers: We have done our best to make sure all Internet Addresses in this book were active and appropriate when we went to press. However, the author and the publisher have no control over and assume no liability for the material available on those Internet sites or on other Web sites they may link to. Any comments or suggestions can be sent by e-mail to comments@enslow.com or to the address on the back cover.

♻ Enslow Publishers, Inc., is committed to printing our books on recycled paper. The paper in every book contains 10% to 30% post-consumer waste (PCW). The cover board on the outside of each book contains 100% PCW. Our goal is to do our part to help young people and the environment too!

Photo Credits: © 2011 Photos.com, a division of Getty Images. All rights reserved, pp. 6, 10, 28; © 2012 Clipart.com, a division of Getty Images, pp. 24, 34, 35; Florida Keys National Marine Sanctuary, 43; © GeoAtlas, p. 4; Jose Cort/NOAA, p. 39; Matt Wilson/Jay Clark, NOAA, p. 25 (left); Mr. Ben Mieremet, Senior Advisor OSD, NOAA, p. 31; ©National Oceanic and Atmospheric Administration (NOAA), pp. 25 (right), 29, 37; Photos.com: Jose Cort/NOAA, p. 41, Olga Khoroshunova, pp. 32, 44; Polina Pomortseva, p. 17; Ralf Hettler, p. 27; Shutterstock.com, pp. 3, 5, 8, 11, 14, 19, 23, 30, 33, 38, and all headers; © Stephen Rountree, p. 20; Shutterstock.com: belizar, p. 16, Paul Cowan, p. 15; This image comes from The Report of the Scientific Results of the Exploring Voyage of H.M.S. *Challenger* during the years 1873-1876 published 1885-95., p. 36; © Tom LaBaff, p. 18; © United States Geological Service (USGS), p. 22; U.S. Navy photo by Mass Communication Specialist Seaman Jesse L. Gonzalez/Released, p. 13.

Cover Credit: Carol Buchanan/Photos.com (clownfish); Shutterstock.com (all others)

Table of
CONTENTS

THE TROPICAL INDIAN OCEAN

EUROPE

ASIA

Mediterranean Sea

Suez Canal

Red Sea

Persian Gulf

AFRICA

Arabian Sea

India

Bay Of Bengal

Andaman Sea

Maldives

Sri Lanka

Seychelles

INDIAN OCEAN

Mid-Indian Ridge

Ninetyeast Ridge

Java Trench

Strait Of Malacca

Madagascar

AUSTRALIA

Southwest Indian Ridge

Southeast Indian Ridge

Great Barrier

TA

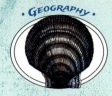

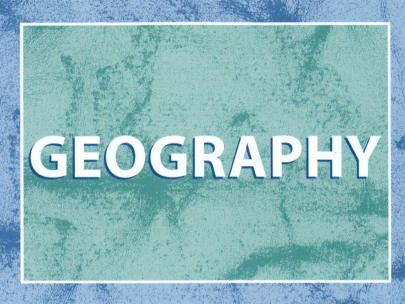

Chapter 1

GEOGRAPHY

The Indian Ocean lies between Africa on the west and Australia and Indonesia on the east. Asia is the ocean's northern boundary. The Southern Ocean borders it to the south.

Most of the Indian Ocean lies in the Southern Hemisphere. It covers over 26 million square miles (68 million square kilometers). It is the third largest ocean on Earth.

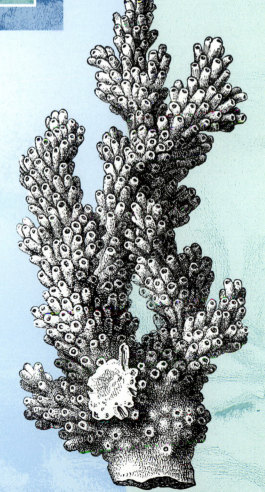

The Indian Ocean

The Ocean That Looks Like an M

The Indian forms a giant M on the surface of the globe. It holds several seas. *Sea* can be another word for ocean. It can also mean a part of an ocean. The Arabian Sea and the Red Sea are both in the Indian Ocean. The Persian Gulf is another large body of water in the Indian.

The Indian Ocean is full of islands. Many are part of the island country of Indonesia. Madagascar is the largest island in the Indian Ocean.

Climate

Much of the Indian Ocean lies within the tropics. The tropics are the areas 1,600 miles (2,575 kilometers) on either side of the equator. The tropics have warm temperatures all year long.

The waters in the tropics stay warm, too. Surface water rarely drops below 70°F (21°C). In July, the temperature of the water can reach up to 90°F (32°C).

The water is cooler south of the tropics. Indian Ocean water also gets colder as it gets deeper. Water in the deepest part of the ocean is near freezing.

Monsoons

A monsoon is a wind that changes direction with the season. From November to March, winds blow southwesterly across the Indian Ocean. In April, the winds change direction. They blow northeasterly across the water and then onto land. This monsoon brings heavy rains to Asia. It is called the wet monsoon.

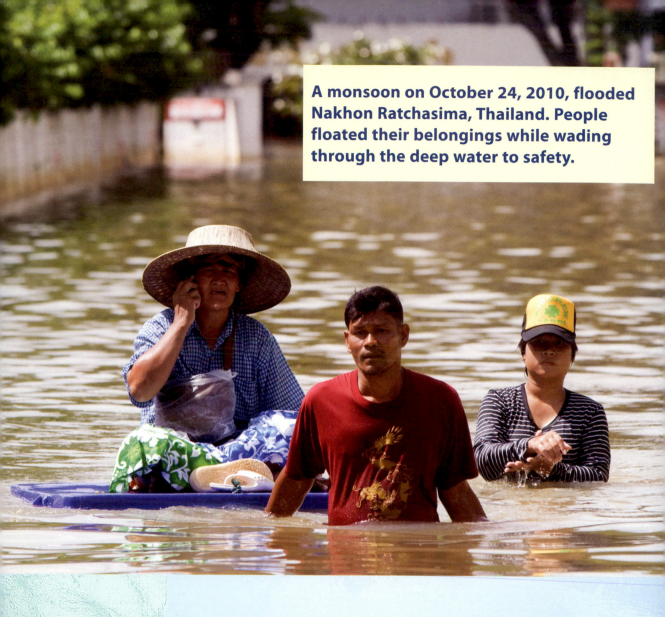

A monsoon on October 24, 2010, flooded Nakhon Ratchasima, Thailand. People floated their belongings while wading through the deep water to safety.

People in India, Bangladesh, and Thailand depend on the monsoon rains. They use the rain for drinking and watering crops. Yet the rains can also be destructive. They can cause floods that ruin property and even cause death.

Cyclones

Sometimes ocean winds grow into cyclones.
A cyclone is a severe storm with whirling winds.
Cyclones are common in the tropical areas of the
Indian Ocean. At times they move onto land.
Like monsoons, cyclones can cause property
damage and death.

Currents

Indian Ocean winds create currents, too.
A current is water that moves in a constant
and regular motion. It is like a river in the sea.

One Indian Ocean current flows westward
along the equator. When it reaches Africa, it flows
south. It then turns and flows east to Australia.
This current is known as the south equatorial
current.

Tides

Ocean waters also move in tides. Tides are caused
by the moon's gravity. When the moon is on one
side of the earth, its gravity pulls the ocean waters
toward the moon. This makes each wave go a little

Winds and currents make it possible to enjoy sailing.

higher onto the land. The water level drops on the part of earth farthest from the moon.

As the earth rotates, the moon pulls on different waters. This water is drawn farther and farther up the shore, and the water that was high now recedes. Because the earth and the moon are constantly moving, the area of high tide is constantly changing. At any one place, tides change twice each day.

Resources from the
INDIAN OCEAN

The Indian Ocean provides humans with many resources. It is also a trade route for shipping goods around the world. In addition, the Indian Ocean is a popular place for tourists to visit.

Oil

The earth below the Indian Ocean is rich in oil and natural gas. Huge drills and pumps are needed to pull them to the surface. These are built on platforms called offshore wells.

Most of the oil from the Indian Ocean comes from deep below the Persian Gulf. This area is the largest oil-producing region on Earth. More than one fourth of all the oil used in the world comes from the countries in the Persian Gulf.

Trade Routes

Most Persian Gulf oil is transported to other countries by way of the Indian Ocean. Many oil tankers sail around the continent of Africa. Others travel to the Pacific Ocean through the Strait of Malacca.

One of the most popular trade routes is through the Suez Canal. The Suez Canal is a man-made waterway. It connects the Red Sea to the Mediterranean Sea.

Other goods are also shipped to cities around the Indian Ocean. The most common of these trade goods are iron, coal, rubber, and tea.

The aircraft carrier USS *Enterprise* moves through the Suez Canal in Egypt. *Enterprise* was doing security operations and providing military support to Operations Enduring Freedom and New Dawn.

Military Base

Some countries have military bases on the Indian Ocean. The United States has one on an island named Diego Garcia, which is near the middle of the ocean. The base there has airstrips for fighter and cargo planes, and harbors for warships and submarines.

Tuna are one of the main catches for fishermen in the Indian Ocean.

Food

The Indian Ocean is an important source of food for the people who live near it. Most fishing is done on small boats. The catch is eaten by the fishers' families or sold in local markets.

Some large fishing ships operate in the Indian Ocean. They mainly catch shrimp and tuna.

Nature's Museum

Some of the rarest animals on earth live on islands in the Indian Ocean. For example, twelve species of birds seen nowhere else in the world live on the islands of Seychelles. Among them are the magpie robin and the black parrot.

The world's seventh most endangered bird, the Seychelles magpie robin lives on Frègate Island in the Indian Ocean. Just over one hundred of these critically endangered birds remain. People are working to help them survive.

The angonoka
tortoise feeds
on grasses
and shrubs.
It lives on
Madagascar,
an island in
the Indian
Ocean.

Another rare species is the angonoka tortoise. It lives on Madagascar. The angonoka grows to 18 inches (46 centimeters) long. There are only about two hundred angonokas living in the wild today.

Tourism

Unusual wildlife, a warm climate, and sandy beaches make some Indian Ocean islands popular vacation spots. The tourism industry is important

to the people who live there. Vacation resorts, shops, and restaurants provide them with jobs. Without tourists, these people might not have any work.

Water Cycle

People everywhere depend on the Indian Ocean in one very basic way: It helps keep the earth supplied with water. Ocean water evaporates, and then condenses to form clouds. When the clouds

The warm climate and sandy beaches are two of the tourist attractions in the Seychelles Islands.

The oceans are a vital part of the earth's water cycle.

become heavy with condensation, the moisture falls to the ground as rain or snow. Some of this precipitation is used. Much of it ends up back in the ocean to continue the cycle. The Indian Ocean plays an important part in keeping the earth's water cycle alive.

clouds where water condenses

sun

EVAPORATION

rain

OCEAN

The OCEAN FLOOR

The average depth of the Indian Ocean is about 13,000 feet (3,960 meters). Yet the entire seafloor is not smooth. It has many features including deep trenches, high mountains, and even volcanoes.

Continental Shelf

The bottom of the Indian Ocean slopes gently from the shore toward the deep ocean. This incline is called the continental shelf. Most of the ocean's continental shelf is about 75 miles

The bottom of the Indian Ocean slopes gently from the shore toward the deep ocean. This gradual incline is called the continental shelf.

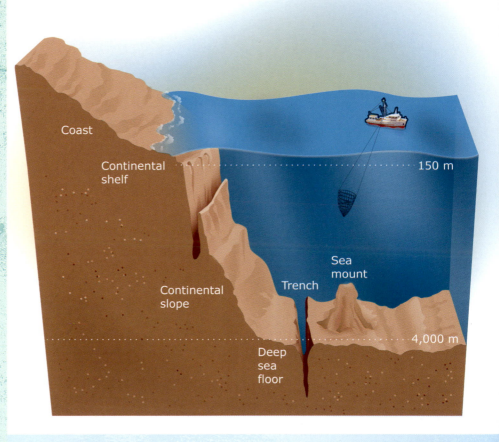

Coast

Continental shelf

150 m

Continental slope

Sea mount

Trench

Deep sea floor

4,000 m

(121 kilometers) long. Between Australia and New Guinea, though, the shelf extends 600 miles (966 kilometers).

The ocean bottom drops sharply at the end of the continental shelf. This steep cliff is called the continental slope. The floor of the deep sea lies at the bottom of the slope.

Several large basins line the floor of the Indian Ocean. A basin is a flat area covered with a thick layer of sand.

Java Trench

Deep channels cut through the basins. These narrow gashes are called trenches. The longest trench in the Indian Ocean is Java Trench. It runs for nearly 1,600 miles (2,575 kilometers) along the western coast of Indonesia.

The deepest place in the Indian Ocean is in Java Trench. It lies 23,812 feet (7,258 meters) below the surface of the sea. This point is called the Sunda Trench.

Mountains

Mountain ranges also run along the ocean bottom. One range is called the Ninetyeast Ridge. It runs from north to south on the eastern side of the ocean.

Another set of ranges forms an upside-down "Y" shape on the ocean floor. The Y-shaped ridge

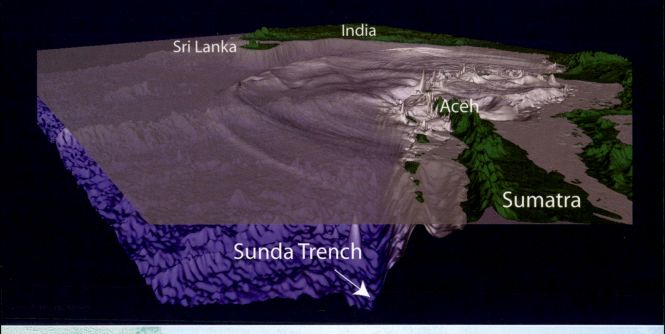

Sri Lanka

India

Aceh

Sumatra

Sunda Trench

An earthquake on December 26, 2004, involved the India plate, which is an oceanic plate and part of the larger Sunda plate. The tsunami wave field in the Bay of Bengal is shown here one hour after the quake.

is part of a longer mountain range called the mid-ocean ridge.

The mid-ocean ridge runs through every ocean in the world. It is important in a theory called plate tectonics. According to plate tectonics, the earth's crust sits on several huge pieces of rock called plates. The mid-ocean ridge runs along the edges of some plates. Powerful forces inside the earth push the plates together and pull them apart.

Earthquakes and Volcanoes

All of the pushing and pulling of plates causes ocean earthquakes and volcanoes. Much of the

time these are not felt on land. Sometimes, though, they trigger huge waves that reach land and cause destruction. These waves are called a tsunami.

In 2004, a huge earthquake near Indonesia set off a deadly tsunami. It moved across the ocean at the speed of an airplane with waves up to 50 feet (15 meters) high. These slammed into coastlines all around the ocean. The force of the waves destroyed buildings and killed more than 150,000 people.

This photo shows damage from the Sumatra tsunami in Sri Lanka.

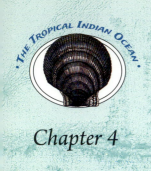
Chapter 4

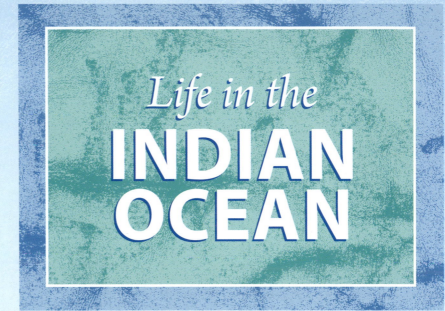

Life in the
INDIAN OCEAN

Many different plants and animals live in the Indian Ocean. Each one depends on several others to survive. A group of plants and animals that need each other is called an ecosystem. The Indian Ocean has several ecosystems.

Plankton

Many animals of the sea cannot swim. Instead, they float about with the ocean's waves and currents. These

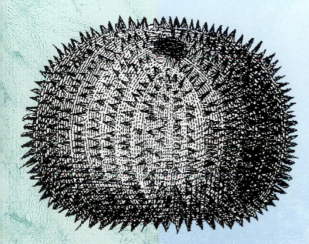

animals are called zooplankton. Most kinds of zooplankton are tiny, but some grow quite large.

The ocean also contains plants that float around. They are called phytoplankton. Seaweeds are large phytoplankton. Other phytoplankton are microscopic.

Together, the phytoplankton and zooplankton make up the plankton. Without plankton, no sea creature would survive. Small plankton are the

Zooplankton (left) are usually tiny and difficult to see with the naked eye. These small ocean animals were photographed under the microscope.

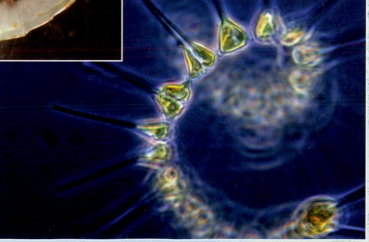

Phytoplankton (right) are very small plants that float in the ocean. They are shown here under a microscope.

food of small animals. These small animals become food for larger ones. The larger animals are then eaten by even larger ones.

Whales

One very large animal eats nothing but tiny plankton. The blue whale is the largest animal on Earth. It can grow 100 feet (30 meters) long. Its favorite food is a small zooplankton called krill.

The blue whale is a baleen whale. Fin and sei whales are other baleen whales of the Indian Ocean. Baleens have thin plates of a bone-like substance inside their mouths called baleen. It is covered with brush-like fibers.

Baleen whales eat by taking in gulps of water. They then push the water out of their mouths, trapping plankton in the baleen.

Toothed whales also live in the Indian Ocean. They have teeth and eat fish. Dolphins and porpoises are the smallest toothed whales of the Indian Ocean.

Fish

The largest fish in the Indian Ocean are the tuna, swordfish, and sailfish. These fish are strong, fast swimmers. This makes them expert predators.

Many kinds of sharks live in the Indian Ocean, too. One of the most dangerous is the great white shark. It can grow twenty feet (six meters) long.

Several species of smaller fish also live in the Indian Ocean. Among them are flying fish, mackerel, and sardine.

Toothed whales include dolphins, porpoises, killer whales (shown here), and sperm whales. They have teeth to catch their slippery prey.

Sardines are just one of many species of small fish that swim in the waters of the Indian Ocean.

Bottom Dwellers

Some animals live on the bottom of the ocean. Many eat decaying plants and animals that float down from above.

Some bottom dwellers have light organs that blink on and off to attract prey. Others have huge mouths that animals swim into without even knowing it.

Birds and Turtles

Several kinds of birds live on or near the Indian. Some spend their days at sea looking for food. Many nest on land at night. Some seabirds

actually live at sea. They come to land once a year to lay eggs and raise babies.

Marine turtles spend most of their time at sea, too. Green turtles are numerous in the Indian Ocean. They can grow up to 650 pounds (295 kilograms). They will swim thousands of miles to nest where they hatched. Green turtles eat ocean plants.

There are many sea turtles in the Indian Ocean.

Dugongs

Another plant eater is the dugong. This mammal lives in warm, coastal waters. It can can be 10 feet (3 meters) long and 650 pounds (295 kilograms).

Dugongs are plant eaters that live in warm, coastal waters.

Dugongs have blunt snouts with bristly whiskers. The males have two upper tusks. They live in small groups. They eat sea grass by pushing it into their mouths with their flippers.

Mangroves

One common plant of the Indian Ocean is the mangrove tree. Mangroves grow in muddy seawater near warm coasts. Their roots grow out of the mud, twisting around each other like a tangled mass of rope.

A mangrove swamp is made up of groups of mangroves. These swamps are filled with birds, crabs, and fish.

One of the strangest fish of the swamps is the mudskipper. The mudskipper uses its fins to crawl out of the ocean and across the shore. There it climbs up mangrove roots and onto branches to rest.

Coral

Another ecosystem in the Indian Ocean is built around the polyp. Polyps are animals that take calcium out of the seawater. They use it to make their own skeletons. When a polyp dies, its body decays, but the skeleton remains.

Polyps are only an inch long. However, they attach themselves to one another to build large structures called coral. Coral can be bright orange,

This mangrove tree is surrounded by coral rock. Mangrove trees grow in warm, muddy water along some Indian Ocean coasts.

purple, and green. It can be shaped like baskets, fans, and fingers.

At times coral grows so big it makes a reef or ridge under the sea. The tropical ocean is filled with coral reefs.

Hundreds of kinds of fish live around coral reefs. Most are brightly colored. Many have stripes or spots. These markings help them blend into their surroundings. Sponges, crabs, sea urchins, and starfish also live around coral.

The tropical Indian Ocean is home to coral reefs.

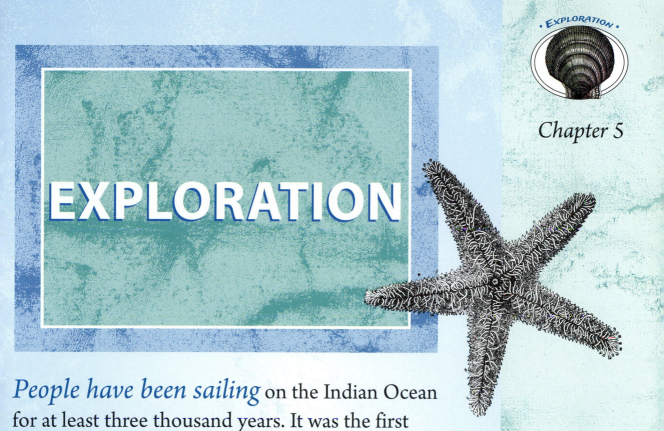

EXPLORATION

People have been sailing on the Indian Ocean for at least three thousand years. It was the first ocean to be used as a trade route.

The First Explorers

The first ocean traders were Arab sailors. They sailed along the East African coast beginning around A.D. 500. They used wooden boats with triangle-shaped sails called dhows. People still travel the Indian in dhows today.

By the early 1400s, people from China, India, and Africa were making frequent voyages on the Indian Ocean.

Explorers From Europe

In 1497, Vasco da Gama left Portugal. He sailed around Africa and then across the Indian Ocean to India. His expedition opened the first all-water trade route from Europe to Asia.

Captain James Cook of Great Britain was the first to explore the farthest southern reaches of the Indian Ocean. He sailed these waters in 1772.

Sailing for the country of Portugal, Italian explorer Vasco da Gama (left) sailed around the southern tip of Africa and into the Indian Ocean.

Captain James Cook of Great Britain (right) explored the southern reaches of the Indian Ocean.

Exploring for Science

The H.M.S. *Challenger* was the first ship sent out on a mission of oceanography. Oceanography is the study of ocean waters and its life.

The *Challenger* left Great Britain in 1872. It spent six months studying the Indian Ocean. *Challenger* scientists learned much about the ocean's temperature and the depths of its basins.

Twentieth-Century Research

From 1940 until 1960, many other ships studied the Indian Ocean. One, the *Challenger II*, measured the depth of the ocean using an echo sounder. This device shot sound waves at the ocean bottom. Scientists then measured how long it took for the sound to return to the surface. They used this number to figure out how far it was to the seafloor.

In 1872, the H.M.S. *Challenger* set sail from Great Britain on a quest to explore the world's oceans. The ship and its crew spent six months researching the Indian Ocean.

These are some different kinds of coral collected aboard the H.M.S. *Challenger*, during the late-nineteenth-century expedition.

The Deep Sea Drilling Project

In 1968, the Deep Sea Drilling Project began. Pipes were pushed deep into the seabed. They were then pulled back up and carefully opened. The insides are called core samples.

Scientists studied the samples. Each one had several different layers. Some contained fossils. Others had grains of pollen in them.

The core samples helped scientists learn more about the geological history of the earth. The oldest seafloor they found was 175 million years old.

In 2003, the Deep Sea Drilling Project was replaced by a new project. This one used tools that could drill 23,000 feet (7,000 meters) into the seafloor.

Research Today

Today oceanographers are researching the ocean's monsoons and currents. Their work could improve weather forecasts.

Marine biologists are also studying Indian Ocean life. One of their most useful tools is the animal cam. This is a tiny camera that is carefully attached to a marine animal. After the animal is released, biologists monitor its movements and actions.

Some scientists are looking for new animal species. They take DNA samples from animals they find and compare them to animals that are already known. This tells scientists whether they have found a new species. New species are being found all the time. This tells researchers that there is still much to learn about the Indian Ocean.

Bubblegum coral, or paragorgiidae, are among the potential new species encountered by the deep sea expedition.

A Healthy
OCEAN

We all depend on the Indian Ocean for something. This makes it important to us all. In many ways, though, the ocean is not healthy.

Oil Pollution

Oil, chemicals, human sewage, and garbage pollute the Indian. Some of these pollutants are dumped into rivers that run to the ocean. Sometimes they are dumped directly into the sea.

It only takes a little pollution to kill plankton. This can change entire ecosystems. Pollutants can also kill

This fishing workboat has just finished surrounding a school of tuna in the western part of the Indian Ocean. Water pollution is a threat to the quality of fish in the ocean, and could put the people that eat the fish in danger of becoming ill.

larger marine plants and animals. Furthermore, the animals that survive pollution are not always safe to eat.

Climate Change

The warming of the earth's climate is also harming the Indian Ocean. Ice in polar regions is melting. This is raising the water level in all the oceans. Indian Ocean islands called the

Sundarbans are already sinking because of rising sea levels. Right now over 4 million people live on these islands. They will all need to find a new place to live. Rising water levels will also change ecosystems.

Warmer temperatures will change ecosystems, too. In some areas of the Indian, warmer temperatures have damaged much of the coral. This will affect the plants and animals that need the coral to live.

In addition to becoming warmer, ocean water is becoming more acidic. This is called acidification. Acidification makes it hard for corals and other marine life to develop.

Overuse

Too much fishing is also damaging the Indian. Fish are caught for food or sold for aquariums. When too many of one kind of fish are taken from an area, other species that depend on it suffer. Overfishing can destroy ecosystems.

Overuse is also damaging coral reefs. These are popular places for people to visit. Sometimes

their boats damage the coral. Worse still, people take hundreds of tons of shells and coral from reefs each year. This disturbs and changes the coral ecosystem.

Disappearing Mangrove Swamps

Many cities near the Indian Ocean are growing. This creates a need for more houses, stores, and schools. Sometimes mangrove swamps are cut down to make room for them. Trees are also cut for lumber and firewood.

Coral reefs are in danger of destruction from people who take coral as souvenirs or fishers who destroy coral with cyanide or explosives.

Cutting mangrove swamps leads to floods. In addition, it destroys the mangrove ecosystem. One half of all the mangrove swamps in the world have already been lost.

Loss of habitat results in loss of species. Without a place to live, an animal population decreases. When a species' numbers drop very low, it is said to be endangered. This means the animal could disappear from the earth forever.

Endangered Species

A number of animals in the Indian Ocean are endangered. They include large whales, the green turtle, and the hawksbill turtle.

The dugong is another endangered species. Development has ruined many of the sea grass beds they need to survive.

Protecting Species

Many countries have made laws against hunting endangered species. People hope that by protecting these species, their numbers will recover.

Some countries have created sea sanctuaries or reserves to protect ocean life. These are places where marine life cannot be disturbed. One of the world's largest marine reserves is in the Indian Ocean.

In the past, people did not always realize that their actions could damage the Indian Ocean forever. Today, though, we do know this. This understanding makes us all responsible for doing what we can to keep the ocean healthy for the future.

Hawksbill sea turtles are endangered. Hawksbills feed mostly on sponges.

INDIAN OCEAN FACTS

🐟 **Area:** About 26,469,6000 square miles (68,556,000 square kilometers)

🐟 **Average Depth:** 13,000 feet (4,000 meters)

🐟 **Greatest Known Depth:** The Sunda Trench in Indonesia 23,812 feet (7,258 meters).

🐟 **Greatest Distances:** North to south is about 6,140 miles (9,880 kilometers). East to west is about 6,200 miles (10,000 kilometers).

🐟 **Surface Temperature:** Highest: About 90°F (32°C) in the Persian Gulf and Red Sea. Lowest: Below 30°F (−1°C) near Antarctic waters.

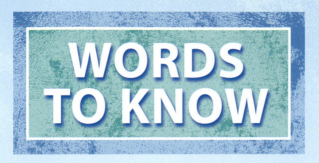

WORDS TO KNOW

acidification—The process of water becoming more acidic, which makes it hard for marine life to grow.

basin—In the ocean, a large bowl-shaped area that is deeper than the surrounding area; basins often have a sandy bottom.

climate—The general weather patterns of a particular area.

continental shelf—The submerged border of a large landmass.

continental slope—The part of the continental shelf that drops off steeply to the ocean floor.

coral reef—A large rocky mass of old coral, sometimes with new coral growing on top.

current—A strong movement of water in one direction.

cyclone—A strong storm of swirling wind and often heavy rain.

dugong—A large mammal that eats plants and lives in warm coastal waters.

It is similar to a manatee but its tail is more like that of a whale.

earthquake—The shaking of part of the earth, usually caused by the movement of the plates.

echo sounder—An instrument that sends out sound signals and measures the time it takes for the signals to bounce back from an object; the time shows how far the object is from the instrument.

endangered—At risk of dying out completely.

equator—The imaginary line that runs around the center of Earth, dividing it equally into the northern and southern hemispheres.

hemisphere—Half a sphere, such as the planet Earth.

mangrove tree—A tree whose roots grow from the trunk at a point above the water. These trees grow close together in salty marshes or other shallow salt water.

mid-ocean ridge—The underwater mountain range that runs through all the oceans of the world.

monsoon—A seasonal wind in the southern Indian Ocean that brings the rainy season.

ocean—The entire body of salt water that covers most of the earth, including the Atlantic Ocean, Pacific Ocean, Indian Ocean, Arctic Ocean, and Southern Ocean.

oil—A thick liquid found deep underground that is the source of gasoline, fuel oils, and other products.

phytoplankton—Plant plankton.

plankton—Tiny plants and animals, phytoplankton and zooplankton, that float in the water.

pollution—Anything such as oil, garbage, and human waste that is not in its proper place.

polyp—A small animal that is shaped like a cylinder and has tentacles around its opening; many polyps live together to form coral.

Suez Canal—The waterway that was built across the tip of Egypt to join the Mediterranean Sea with the Red Sea, which empties into the Indian Ocean.

tide—The regular rise or fall of sea level, caused by the moon's pull on Earth's surface. There are usually two high tides and two low tides each day.

tourism—The business of keeping a country's visitors entertained.

trade route—A sea lane used by ships that carry goods for buying or selling.

trench—A deep gash through an ocean basin.

tropics—The area of Earth on either side of the equator, between the Tropic of Cancer and the Tropic of Capricorn; the climate there is generally hot and often rainy.

tsunami—An extremely large wave caused by an earthquake.

volcano—A hole or crack in Earth's surface where rocks, lava, and hot gases can escape; a mountain that was formed by escaped rocks and lava.

water cycle—The series that Earth's water goes through, from clouds to rain or snow to rivers and oceans and then back again.

zooplankton—Animal plankton.

LEARN MORE

BOOKS

Benoit, Peter. *Oceans*. New York: Children's Press, 2011.

Callery, Sean. *Life Cycles: Ocean*. New York: Kingfisher, 2011.

Johnson, Jinny. *Coral Reef Life*. Mankato, Minn.: Smart Apple Media, 2012.

Kalman, Bobbie. *Explore Earth's Five Oceans*. New York: Crabtree Pub. Company, 2010.

Roza, Greg. *The Indian Ocean Tsunami*. New York: PowerKids Press, 2007.

Ylvisaker, Anne. *The Indian Ocean*. Mankato, Minn.: Capstone Press, 2006.

WEB SITES

CIA World Factbook. *Oceans: Indian Ocean.* <http://www.cia.gov/library/publications/the-world-factbook/geos/xo.html>

National Geographic. *The Ocean.* <http://ocean.nationalgeographic.com/ocean>

INDEX